Lektürewortschatz zu Crooked Letter, Crooked Letter

von Lena Missel

Ernst Klett Sprachen
Stuttgart

1. Auflage   1 ⁵ ⁴ ³ ² ¹ | 2022 21 20 19 18

Alle Drucke dieser Auflage sind unverändert und können im Unterricht nebeneinander verwendet werden.
Die letzte Zahl bezeichnet das Jahr des Druckes. Das Werk und seine Teile sind urheberrechtlich geschützt. Jede Nutzung in anderen als den gesetzlich zugelassenen Fällen bedarf der vorherigen schriftlichen Einwilligung des Verlags. Hinweis zu § 52 a UrhG: Weder das Werk noch seine Teile dürfen ohne eine solche Einwilligung eingescannt und in ein Netzwerk eingestellt werden. Dies gilt auch für Intranets von Schulen und sonstigen Bildungseinrichtungen. Fotomechanische oder andere Wiedergabeverfahren nur mit Genehmigung des Verlags.

© Ernst Klett Sprachen GmbH, Rotebühlstraße 77, 70178 Stuttgart 2018
Alle Rechte vorbehalten.
www.klett-sprachen.de

Autorin: Lena Missel
Redaktion: Debby Böhm
unter Mitarbeit von: Evelyn Zehren, Lisa Stephan
Layoutkonzeption: Maja Merz
Gestaltung und Satz: Datagroup Int. SRL, Timisoara, Rumänien
Umschlaggestaltung: Greta Gröttrup
Titelbild: shutterstock / Rene Jansa / Bukhavets Mikhail, New York, NY
Illustration S. 24: Shutterstock (okili77), New York
Druck und Bindung: Medienhaus Plump GmbH, Rheinbreitbach

Printed in Germany
ISBN 978-3-12-579905-9

Inhaltsverzeichnis

1 Major themes and motifs
1.1 The ambiguity of belonging — 6
1.1.1 Belonging — 6
1.1.2 Community — 8
1.1.3 Family — 11
1.1.4 Love and friendship — 12
1.2 Gender roles — 15
1.2.1 Male stereotypes — 15
1.2.2 Men in the novel — 16
1.2.3 Women in the novel — 16
1.3 Crime and legal terms — 17

2 Setting
2.1 The American South — 24
2.2 Historical background — 27
2.3 Surroundings — 34
2.3.1 Mood and ambience — 34
2.3.2 Housing — 35
2.3.3 Flora and fauna — 35
2.4 Occupations and workplaces — 37
2.4.1 Police — 37
2.4.2 Ottomotive Repair — 38
2.4.3 Hospital — 38
2.4.4 Journalism — 40

3 Characterization
3.1 General terms — 41
3.2 Main characters — 43
3.2.1 Larry Ott — 43
3.2.2 Silas Jones — 47
3.2.3 Wallace Stringfellow — 49
3.3 Side characters — 50
3.3.1 Cindy Walker — 50
3.3.2 Cecil Walker — 51
3.3.3 Ina Ott — 52
3.3.4 Carl Ott — 53
3.3.5 Alice Jones — 54
3.3.6 Angie — 55
3.3.7 Roy French — 56

4 Literary terms
4.1 Genre — 57
4.2 Talking about a book — 58
4.3 Stylistic devices — 62

Liebe Leserinnen und Leser,

der vorliegende **Lektürewortschatz zu *Crooked Letter, Crooked Letter*,** thematisch in vier Kapitel unterteilt, bietet Ihnen ein unerlässliches Hilfsmittel für die mündliche und schriftliche Auseinandersetzung mit dem Roman. Mithilfe der überschaubaren, sinnvoll zusammengestellten Lernportionen erweitern Sie Ihren Wortschatz um verlässliches Vokabular zu allen wichtigen Themen und Motiven des Romans. Mit dem Lektürewortschatz sind Sie somit bestens ausgerüstet, *Crooked Letter, Crooked Letter* im Unterricht zu erarbeiten.

Viel Erfolg und Freude bei der Lektüre wünscht Ihnen
Die Redaktion Englisch, Ernst Klett Sprachen GmbH

Übersicht über die verwendeten Symbole und Abkürzungen

adj	adjective	Adjektiv
adv	adverb	Adverb
AE	American English	amerikanisches Englisch
BE	British English	britisches Englisch
coll	colloquial	umgangssprachlich
derog	derogative	abwertend
etw		etwas
FF	false friend	falscher Freund (ein Wort, das nicht das bedeutet, was man vom Deutschen her erwarten könnte.)
jd, jdn, jdm, jds		jemand, jemanden, jemandem, jemandes
n	noun	Nomen, Substantiv
pl	plural	Plural
prep	preposition	Präposition
sb	somebody	(irgend) jemand
sing	singular	Singular
sth	something	etwas
uncount	uncountable (noun)	nicht zählbar(es Nomen)
v	verb	Verb
=	synonym (same meaning)	Synonym
≠	antonym (opposite meaning)	Antonym
▶	words in the same word family	Hinweis auf Wörter der gleichen Familie

Alle phonemischen Transkriptionen entsprechen gängigem amerikanischem Englisch, basierend auf Einträgen der Website www.pons.com.

Lektürewortschatz zu *Crooked Letter, Crooked Letter* auf einen Blick

> Deckt Themen ab, die im Kontext von *Crooked Letter, Crooked Letter* relevant und wichtig sind.

1 MAJOR THEMES AND MOTIFS

1.1 The ambiguity of belonging

1.1.1 Belonging

ambiguity [ˌæmbəˈgjuːəti] *n* — Doppeldeutigkeit, Unklarheit
belong *v* — dazugehören
  belong together — zusammengehören
  put sth back where it belongs — etw dahin zurücklegen, wo es hingehört
belonging(ness) *n* — Zugehörigkeit
  = affiliation
basic needs *n, pl* — Grundbedürfnisse
vital [ˈvaɪtᵊl] *adj* — lebensnotwendig, essenziell
  play a vital part — eine entscheidende Rolle spielen
inclusion [ɪnˈkluːʒᵊn] *n* — Einbeziehung, Inklusion
  social inclusion
social life *n*

Synonyme (=) / Antonyme (≠)

cohesion [koʊˈhiːʒᵊn] *n*
identity *n*

Maslow's hierarchy of needs
Maslowsche Bedürfnis[...]

- self-actualization — Selbstverwirklichung
- self-esteem — Selbstwertgefühl
- social belonging — *hier:* soziale Bedürfnisse
- security — Sicherheit
- physical n[...] körperli[...]

> Infoboxen zu ausgewählten Themen

> Mindmaps visualisieren wichtige Wortschatzthemen

1 MAJOR THEMES AND MOTIFS

Gun ownership in the U.S.

The U.S. has the highest **gun ownership** rate in the world. Although people claim they only possess a gun to feel more secure or use it for self-defense, possessing **firearms** does not increase security. The U.S. suffers from **mass shootings** much more often than any other **developed country** – and the rate has been increasing in recent years. Unfortunately, the government has not adequately **responded to** these **developments**. Tougher **regulations** and **gun control laws** are **prohibited** by lobbyists and are not currently a priority for the Republican Party.

gun ownership *n* — Waffenbesitz
  = possession of firearms
  ▸ own — ▸ besitzen
arms *n, pl* — Waffen
  = firearms — Schusswaffen
mass shooting *n* — Massenschießerei
developed country *n* — Industriestaat
respond to a development *v* — auf eine Entwicklung reagieren
regulation *n* — Bestimmung, Vorschrift
gun control laws *n* — Reglementierung des Waffenbesitzes
prohibit *v* — verhindern, verbieten

> Hinweise auf Wortfamilien

weapon *n* — Waffe
rifle [ˈraɪfl] *n* — Gewehr
gun [gʌn] *n* — Feuerwaffe (Kanone, Gewehr, Pistole)
bullet [ˈbʊlɪt] *n* — (Gewehr-, Pistolen-)Kugel
cartridge *n* — Patrone
calibre *n* — Kaliber
lever [ˈlevə, ˈliːvə] *n* — (Lade-)Hebel
cock *v* — spannen
  to cock a gun — ein Gewehr spannen, eine Waffe entsichern
aim [eɪm] *n, v* — Ziel, zielen
  take aim at sb / sth — auf jdn / etw zielen
  aim a gun at sb / sth — ein Gewehr auf jdn / etw richten
  Don't aim that gun at me. — Ziele nicht mit dem Gewehr auf mich.

> Überschaubare, sinnvoll zusammengestellte Lernportionen

> Nützliche Beispielsätze

23

5

1 MAJOR THEMES AND MOTIFS

1.1 The ambiguity of belonging

1.1.1 Belonging

ambiguity [ˌæmbəˈgjuːəṭi] *n*	**Doppeldeutigkeit, Unklarheit**
belong *v*	**dazugehören**
belong together	zusammengehören
put sth back where it belongs	etw dahin zurücklegen, wo es hingehört
belonging(ness) *n*	**Zugehörigkeit**
= affiliation	
basic needs *n, pl*	**Grundbedürfnisse**
vital [ˈvaɪṭəl] *adj*	**lebensnotwendig, essenziell**
play a vital part	eine entscheidende Rolle spielen
inclusion [ɪnˈkluːʒən] *n*	**Einbeziehung, Inklusion**
social inclusion	gesellschaftliche Inklusion
social life *n*	**Privatleben, soziales Zusammenleben**
social cohesion [koʊˈhiːʒən] *n*	**sozialer Zusammenhalt**
(social) identity *n*	**(soziale) Identität**

MAJOR THEMES AND MOTIFS 1

physical contact *n*	Körperkontakt
intimacy *n*	Intimität, Vertrautheit
‣ intimate	‣ eng, vertraut
interaction *n*	Interaktion,
acceptance *n*	Akzeptanz
to meet with (general) acceptance	(allgemein) anerkannt werden, (allgemeine) Anerkennung finden
self-acceptance *n*	Selbstwertgefühl, Selbstannahme
≠ self-denial	≠ Selbstverleugnung
reassured *adj*	beruhigt, bestätigt
bond *n*	Bindung
bond between mother and child	Bindung zwischen Mutter und Kind
find one's calling *v*	seine Berufung finden
self-fulfilling prophecy *n*	selbsterfüllende Prophezeiung

individual *n*	Individuum, (selbstständige) Persönlichkeit
‣ individual *adj*	‣ individuell, einzeln
personality *n*	Persönlichkeit
unique [juːˈniːk] *adj*	einzigartig
society *n*	Gesellschaft
anonymity [ˌænəˈnɪməti] *n*	Anonymität
‣ anonymous [əˈnɑːnəməs]	‣ anonym
uniform *adj*	einheitlich
mainstream *adj*	populär, massenkompatibel

fail *v*	versagen, scheitern, missglücken
‣ failure	‣ Scheitern, Versagen, Misserfolg
uprooted *adj*	entwurzelt, aus der gewohnten Umgebung herausgerissen
vulnerable *adj*	verletzlich
dread sb, sth *v*	jdn, etw fürchten
= fear sb, sth	
= be afraid of sb, sth	
tension [ˈtenʃən] *n*	Spannung
alienation [ˌeɪliəˈneɪʃən] *n*	Entfremdung, Isoliertheit

1 MAJOR THEMES AND MOTIFS

rejection *n*	**Ablehnung**
hostility [hɑːsˈtɪləti] *n*	**Feindseligkeit, Ablehnung**
hostilities [hɑːsˈtɪlətiz] *n, pl, form*	**Feindseligkeiten, Kämpfe**
isolation [ˌaɪsəˈleɪʃᵊn] *n, uncount*	**Isolation, Zurückgezogenheit**
live in total isolation	in völliger Abgeschiedenheit leben
social isolation	soziale Isolation
ostracism *n*	**Ächtung**
▸ to ostracize sb	▸ jdn ächten, verbannen

1.1.2 Community

community *n*	**Gesellschaft, Gemeinschaft, Allgemeinheit, Gemeinde**
the business community	die Geschäftswelt, die Geschäftsleute
the Christian community	die christliche Gemeinde
the local community	die hiesige Gemeinde
member *n*	**Mitglied**
common ground *n*	**Gemeinsamkeit**
traditions *n*	**Traditionen, Bräuche**
= customs	
categories *n*	**Kategorien**
religion [rɪˈlɪdʒᵊn] *n*	**Religion**
practise one's religion	seine Religion ausüben
peer group *n*	**Peergroup, Gruppe Gleichaltriger**
be in sb's year at school *v*	**mit jdm in einer Klasse, einem Jahrgang sein**
team [tiːm] *n*	**Team, Mannschaft**
national team	Nationalmannschaft

sense of community *n*	**Gemeinschaftsgefühl**
feeling of belonging *n*	**Zugehörigkeitsgefühl**
protection *n*	**Schutz**
integrate sb / sth (into sth) [ˈɪntəgreɪt] *v*	**jdn / etw (in etw) integrieren**
feel at ease *v*	**wohl fühlen**
open up *v*	**sich öffnen**

MAJOR THEMES AND MOTIFS 1

differentiation *n*	**Abgrenzung**
▸ differentiate	▸ unterscheiden, einen Unterschied machen, differenzieren
exclude sb from sth [eksˈkluːd] *v*	**jdn von etw ausschließen**
excluded from society	von der Gesellschaft ausgeschlossen
prejudice (against sb) [ˈpredʒədɪs] *n*	**Vorurteil (gegen jdn)**
discriminate against sb [dɪˈskrɪmɪneɪt] *v*	**jdn diskriminieren**
superior (to sb) [səˈpɪriɚ] *adj*	**(jdm) überlegen**
inferior (to sb) [ɪnˈfɪriɚ] *adj*	**(jdm) unterlegen, (jdm) untergeordnet**

leader *n*	**Anführer(in), Leiter(in)**
follower *n*	**Mitläufer**
outsider *n*	**Außenseiter**
join the club *v*	**in die Gruppe aufgenommen werden, eintreten**
test of courage *n*	**Mutprobe**
be born into *v*	**hineingeboren werden in**
relations [rɪˈleɪʃ(ə)nz] *n, pl*	**Beziehungen**
public relations (PR)	Öffentlichkeitsarbeit
interpersonal (or human) relations	zwischenmenschliche Beziehungen
relationship *n*	**Beziehung, Verhältnis**
He has a good relationship with his parents.	Er hat ein gutes Verhältnis zu seinen Eltern.

1 MAJOR THEMES AND MOTIFS

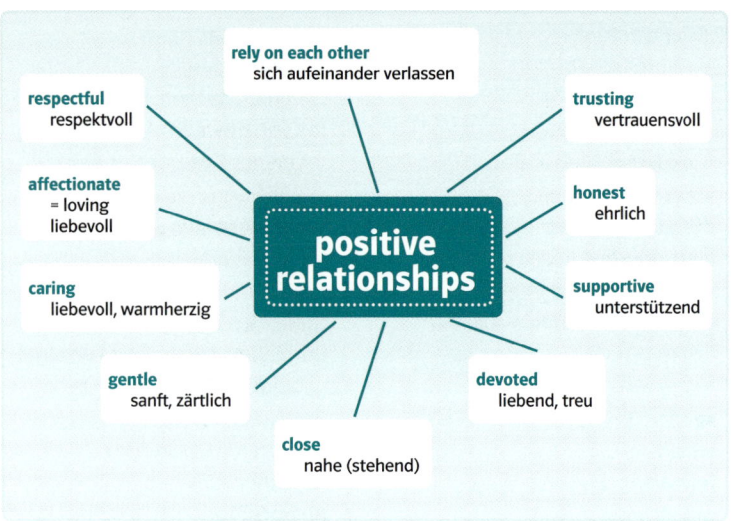

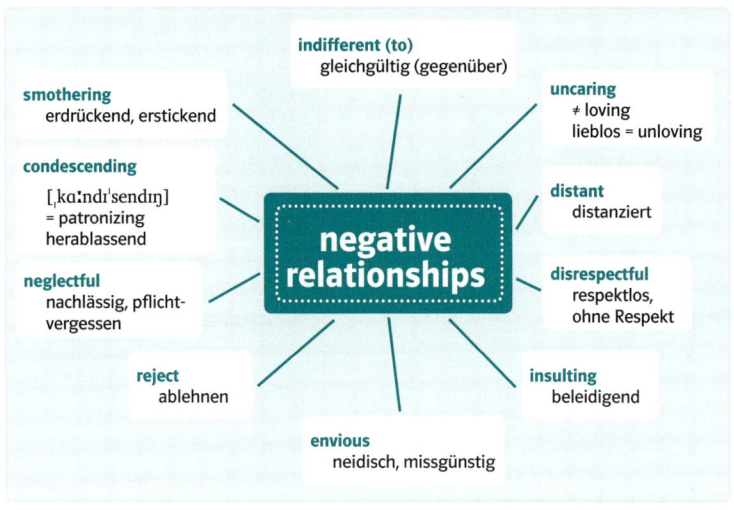

MAJOR THEMES AND MOTIFS 1

1.1.3 Family

family structure *n*	**Familienstruktur**
nuclear family	Kernfamilie
extended family	Großfamilie
patchwork family	Patchworkfamilie
dysfunctional family [dɪsˈfʌŋ(k)ʃənəl] *n*	**Problemfamilie, dysfunktionale Familie**
marriage [ˈmerɪdʒ] *n*	**Ehe**
same-sex marriage	gleichgeschlechtliche Ehe
happy marriage	glückliche Ehe
The marriage fell apart.	Die Ehe ging auseinander.
spouse [spaʊs] *n*	**(Ehe-) Partner(in)**
wife	**(Ehe-)Frau, Gattin**
husband	**(Ehe-)Mann, Gatte**
parent [ˈperənt] *n*	**Elternteil**
birth parents	leibliche Eltern
single parent [ˌsɪŋɡəlˈperənt] *n*	**Alleinerziehende(r)**
mother [ˈmʌðər] *n*	**Mutter**
working mother	berufstätige Mutter
expectant mother	werdende Mutter
maternal [məˈtɜːrnəl] *adj*	**mütterlich, mütterlicherseits, Mutter-**
maternal grandmother	Großmutter mütterlicherseits
maternal feelings	Muttergefühle
father [ˈfɑːðər] *n*	**Vater**
biological father	leiblicher Vater
step father	Stiefvater
absent father	abwesender, fehlender Vater
paternal [pəˈtɜːrnəl] *adj*	**väterlich, väterlicherseits, Vater-**
paternal grandfather	Großvater väterlicherseits
paternal role	Vaterrolle
father-son relationship *n*	**Vater-Sohn-Beziehung**

---

siblings [ˈsɪblɪŋz] *n, pl*	**Geschwister**
half-brother/half-sister *n*	**Halbbruder/Halbschwester**
descent [dɪˈsent] *n*	**Abstammung**
relative [ˈrelətɪv] *n*	**Verwandte(r)**
distant relative	entfernte(r) Verwandte(r)
close relative	nahe(r) Verwandte(r)

1 MAJOR THEMES AND MOTIFS

kinship n	**Verwandschaft, Blutsverwandschaft, nahe Verwandschaft**
▸ degree of kinship (*also: degree of relationship*)	▸ Verwandtschaftsgrad
related to sb [rɪˈleɪt̬ɪd] v	**mit jdm verwandt**
be closely related to sb	mit jdm nah verwandt sein
distantly related	entfernt verwandt

upbringing [ˈʌpˌbrɪŋɪŋ] n, sing	**(familiäre) Erziehung**
well-brought-up adj	**gut erzogen**
≠ badly-brought-up	≠ schlecht erzogen
childhood [ˈtʃaɪldhʊd] n	**Kindheit**
my childhood home	das Haus meiner Kindheit
childhood dream	Kindheitstraum
teen n	**Teenager**
adolescent [ˌædəˈlesᵊnt] n	**Jugendliche(r), Heranwachsende(r)**
puberty [ˈpjuːbət̬i] n, uncount	**Pubertät**
minor n	**Minderjährige(r)**

1.1.4 Love and friendship

love [lʌv] n	**Liebe**
be in love with sb	in jdn verliebt sein
fall in love with sb	sich in jdn verlieben
make love with sb	mit jdm Liebe machen
ask sb out [ˈæskˌaʊt] phrasal v	**jdn zu einem Date einladen**
I'd like to ask her out.	Ich würde gerne mit ihr ausgehen.
date [deɪt] n	**Verabredung, Date**
lunch date	Verabredung zum Mittagessen
blind date	Blind Date
romantic date	romantisches Date
go on a date (with sb)	(mit jdm) ausgehen, ein Date (mit jdm) haben
ask sb on a date	jdn um ein Date bitten, sich mit jdm verabreden
couple [ˈkʌpᵊl] n	**Paar**

MAJOR THEMES AND MOTIFS 1

fidelity *n*	**Treue**
affair [əˈfer] *n*	**Affäre, Seitensprung**
arouse *v*	**erregen**
be aroused	erregt sein
▸ arousal	▸ (sexuelle) Erregung
desire *n*	**(sinnliche) Begierde**
= arousal	
awaken sb's desire	jds Verlangen wecken
arouse sb's desire	jds Verlangen wecken
curb sb's desire	jds Verlangen zügeln
neck *v (coll)*	**knutschen**

---

friendship [ˈfrenʃɪp] *n*	**Freundschaft**
out of friendship	aus Freundschaft (zu jdm)
share (sth with sb) [ʃer] *v*	**(etw mit jdm) teilen**
share one's food	sein Essen teilen
share an apartment, a room (AE)	zusammenwohnen, sich eine Wohnung teilen
share sb's views	der gleichen Ansicht sein wie jd
share one's life with sb	mit jdm sein Leben verbringen
shared secret	gemeinsames Geheimnis
stand up for sb *v*	**für jemanden eintreten**
trust (sb / sth) [trʌst] *v*	**(jdm / etw) vertrauen, (jdm / etw) trauen, Vertrauen haben (in jdn / etw)**
trust in sb / sth	in jdn / etw Vertrauen haben, in jdn / etw vertrauen
trust sb with sth	jdm etw anvertrauen
fully trust sb	jdm komplett vertrauen
I trust your judgement.	Ich traue deinem Urteilsgefühl.
similarity *n*	**Ähnlichkeit**
chatter *v*	**plappern, schwätzen**
▸ chatterbox	▸ Plappermaul
emulate sb *v*	**jdm nacheifern**
comfortable *adj*	**gut, angenehm**

1 MAJOR THEMES AND MOTIFS

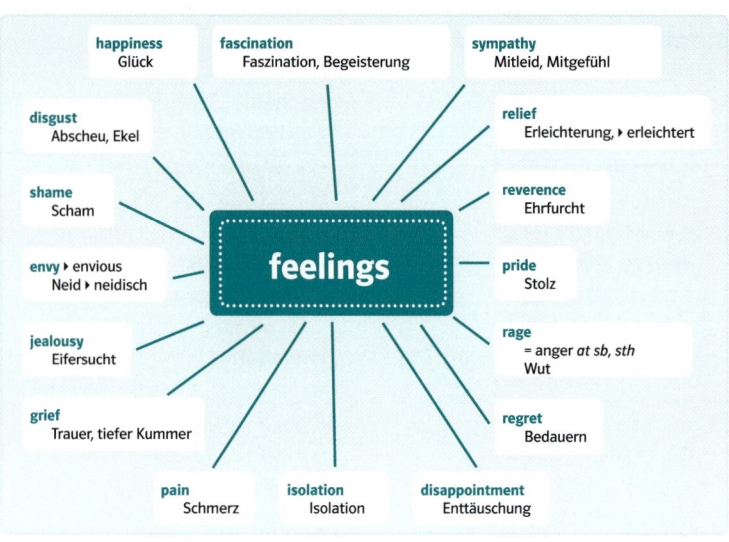

Words expressing emotions

chuckle *v*	kichern
smirk *v*	grinsen
hum *v*	summen
blush *v*	erröten, rot werden
yell [jel] *v*	gellend schreien
shriek [ʃriːk] *v*	kreischen
shriek with laughter	vor Lachen brüllen
wince *v*	(zusammen-)zucken
cry *v*	weinen, rufen
grunt *v*	grunzen, ächzen
frown [fraʊn] *v*	Stirn runzeln, finster dreinblicken

MAJOR THEMES AND MOTIFS 1

1.2 Gender roles

1.2.1 Male stereotypes

gender role *n*	Geschlechterrolle
= sex role	
typical gender role	typische Geschlechterrolle
deviate from classical gender roles	von der klassischen Rollenverteilung (der Geschlechter) abweichen
Jeanne d'Arc tried to overcome the traditional gender role of women.	Jeanne d'Arc versuchte, die klassische Geschlechterrolle der Frau zu überwinden.
role model *n*	**Rollenbild, Vorbild**
= idol [ˈaɪdəl]	
= example	
to serve as an example for sb	jdm als Vorbild dienen
masculine [ˈmæskjəlɪn] *adj*	**männlich, Männer-**
≠ feminine	≠ weiblich
manliness *n*	**Männlichkeit**
virile [ˈvɪrəl] *adj*	**männlich, potent**
testicles *n*	**Hoden**

---

muscular *adj*	muskulös
invincible *adj*	unbesiegbar
strong [strɑːŋ] *adj*	kräftig, stark
firm *adj*	standhaft, robust
able [ˈeɪbəl] *adj*	fähig, kompetent
competitive *adj*	wetteifernd, kompetitiv, leistungsorientiert
stoic [ˈstoʊɪk] *adj*	stoisch, ruhig, gelassen
hide emotions *v*	Gefühle verbergen

---

dominion *n*	Herrschaftsgebiet
man of the house *n*	Hausherr
patriarch *n*	Familienoberhaupt
breadwinner *n*	Brotverdiener, Versorger
provider [prəˈvaɪdɚ] *n*	**Versorger, Provider, Dienstleister**
handy [ˈhændi] *adj* , FF	**praktisch, nützlich**

1 MAJOR THEMES AND MOTIFS

handyman [ˈhændimæn, ˈhændimən] *n* Handwerker; Heimwerker

1.2.2 Men in the novel

racist [ˈreɪsɪst] *adj*	rassistisch
sexist *adj*	sexistisch
fighter *n*	Kämpfer
aggresive *adj*	aggresiv
vulgar [ˈvʌlgɚ] *adj*	vulgär
a vulgar joke	ein geschmackloser Witz
rough [rʌf] *adj*	roh, grob
impulsive *adj*	impulsiv
drinking [ˈdrɪŋkɪŋ] *n*	das Trinken
have a drinking problem	ein Alkoholproblem haben
drinking and driving	Alkohol am Steuer

dominant *adj*	dominant, durchsetzungsfähig
= assertive	
(feeling of) superiority *n*	Überlegenheits(gefühl)
old-fashioned *adj*	antiquiert
= antiquated	
sinister *adj*	finster
stern *adj*	ernst, streng
= strict	

indifferent *adj*	gleichgültig, ungerührt
dissatisfied *adj*	unzufrieden
helpless *adj*	hilflos
derogative *adj*	abwertend
withdrawn *adj*	zurückgezogen

1.2.3 Women in the novel

independent [ˌɪndɪˈpendənt] *adj*	unabhängig, selbständig
≠ dependent *(on)*	≠ abhängig (von)
strong-willed *adj*	eigensinnig, willensstark
▸ strength	▸ Kraft, Stärke

MAJOR THEMES AND MOTIFS

tough [tʌf] *adj*	**unnachgiebig, widerstandsfähig**
be tough on sb / sth	sehr streng und unnachgiebig mit jdm / etw sein
tough and uncompromising	knallhart
She's one tough cookie.	Sie ist ein zäher Typ.
determined [dɪˈtɜːrmɪnd] *adj*	**entschlossen**
I was determined to do better this time.	Ich war fest entschlossen, es diesmal besser zu machen.
assertive *adj*	**durchsetzungsfähig, selbstsicher**
guts [gʌts] *n, inform*	**Mut**
have the guts to do sth	den Mut für etw haben
It takes guts to stand up to an enemy.	Es braucht Mut, sich einem Feind entgegenzustellen.
courageous [kəˈreɪdʒəs] *adj*	**mutig**
a courageous decision	eine mutige Entscheidung
powerful *adj*	**kräftig, energisch, dynamisch**
ambitious [æmˈbɪʃəs] *adj*	**ehrgeizig, anspruchsvoll**

endure sth [enˈdʊr] *v*	**etw ertragen, aushalten**
enduring *adj*	**beständig**
responsible *adj*	**verantwortungsvoll, verantwortlich**

successful [səkˈsesfəl] *adj*	**erfolgreich**
protective *adj*	**beschützend**
show emotions *v*	**Gefühle zeigen**
▸ emotional	

1.3 Crime and legal terms

the **law** [lɑː] *n, sing*	**das Gesetz, das Recht(ssystem)**
break the law	das Gesetz brechen
violate the law	gegen das Gesetz verstoßen
legal [ˈliːgəl] *adj*	**legal; rechtlich, juristisch**
≠ illegal [ɪˈliːgəl]	≠ rechtswidrig, ungesetzlich, illegal
jurisdiction *n*	**Jurisdiktion, Rechtsprechung**
justice *n*	**Gerechtigkeit, Justiz**

1 MAJOR THEMES AND MOTIFS

injustice *n*	Ungerechtigkeit
▸ unjust	▸ ungerecht
trial *n*	Prozess, Gerichtsverhandlung

judge *n*	Richter
▸ judge sb	▸ jdn be-, verurteilen
jury *n*	die Geschworenen
defendant *n*	Angeklagte(r)
convict *n*	Strafgefangene(r), Verurteilte(r)
lawyer *n*	Anwalt
= attorney *AE*	

allegation *n*	Behauptung, Beschuldigung
target sb [ˈtɑːrgɪt] *v*	jmdn. ins Visier nehmen
▸ target	▸ Ziel(scheibe)
accuse sb of sth [əˈkjuːz] *v*	jdn wegen etw anklagen, jdn einer Sache beschuldigen
the accused	der Angeklagte, die Angeklagte
convict (sb) *v*	(jdn) verurteilen
conviction [kənˈvɪkʃ°n] *n*	Verurteilung
sentence sb to sth [ˈsentəns] *v*	jdn zu etw verurteilen
He was sentenced to three years' imprisonment for money laundering.	Er wurde wegen Geldwäsche zu drei Jahren Gefängnis verurteilt.
acquit sb *v*	jdn freisprechen
acquitted	freigesprochen, entlastet
▸ acquittal	▸ Freispruch
exonerate *v*	entlasten, freisprechen
drop a case *v*	einen Fall einstellen

premeditated [ˌpriːˈmedɪteɪtɪd] *adj*	vorsätzlich, geplant
pretense *n*	Vorwand, Vortäuschung
allegedly *adv*	angeblich
probation *n*	Bewährung
self-inflicted *adj*	selbstverschuldet
preliminary *adj*	vorläufig

MAJOR THEMES AND MOTIFS 1

confess [kənˈfes] *v* — zugeben, gestehen
▸ confession — ▸ Geständnis, Beichte
admit sth *v* — etw zugeben
own up to sth *v* — etw zugeben, eingestehen
deny sth [dɪˈnaɪ] *v* — etw leugnen, etw bestreiten
  deny the allegations — die Vorwürfe bestreiten
  ▸ denial — ▸ Ablehnung, Weigerung
plead [pliːd] *v* — plädieren, behaupten, bitten, flehen
  plead guilty (not guilty) — sich schuldig (nicht schuldig) bekennen
  plead for forgiveness, justice, mercy — um Verzeihung, Gerechtigkeit, Gnade bitten

bail *v* — bürgen
  to bail sb out — jdn durch Kaution, gegen Bürgschaft freibekommen
  ▸ bail *n* — ▸ Kaution
guilty [ˈɡɪlti] *adj* — schuldig
  be guilty of an offence — einer Straftat schuldig sein
  They were found guilty of high treason. — Sie wurden des Hochverrats für schuldig befunden.
innocent [ˈɪnəsənt] *adj* — unschuldig
  be innocent of a crime — eines Verbrechens unschuldig sein

emerge *v* — herauskommen, sich herausstellen, an den Tag kommen
  No new evidence emerged during the police investigation. — Durch die polizeiliche Untersuchung kam kein neues Beweismaterial an den Tag.

---

witness *n* — Zeuge, Zeugin
testimony *n* — (Zeugen)aussage
testify *v* — eine Aussage machen
evidence [ˈevɪdəns] *n no pl* — Beweismaterial; beweiskräftige Aussage
  evidence against — Beweise gegen jdn
  give evidence in court — vor Gericht eine Aussage machen

1 MAJOR THEMES AND MOTIFS

print *n*	**Spur, Abdruck**
fingerprint	Fingerabdruck
tire (AE) tyre (BE) prints	Reifenspuren, -abdrücke

warning *n*	**Warnung, Abmahnung, Verwarnung**
warrant *n*	**Haftbefehl**
search warrant	Durchsuchungsbefehl
arrest sb (for sth) [əˈrest] *v*	**jdn (wegen etw) verhaften**
arrest *n*	**Festnahme, Verhaftung**
arrest warrant	Haftbefehl
jail [dʒeɪl] *n*	**Gefängnis, Knast**
prison [ˈprɪzᵊn] *n*	**Gefängnis**
prison cell	Gefängniszelle
He was sent to prison for selling drugs.	Er kam wegen Drogenhandel ins Gefängnis.
prisoner [ˈprɪzᵊnɚ] *n*	**Strafgefangene(r), Häftling**
imprison sb (for sth) [ɪmˈprɪzᵊn] *v*	**jdn (für etw) inhaftieren**
incarcerate *v*	**einsperren**

victim [ˈvɪktɪm] *n*	**Opfer** *(eines Verbrechens)*
crime [kraɪm] *n*	**Verbrechen**
commit a crime	ein Verbrechen begehen
be guilty of a crime	eines Verbrechens schuldig sein
at the crime scene	am Tatort
violent crime	Gewaltverbrechen, Gewaltkriminalität
criminal [ˈkrɪmɪnᵊl] *adj*	**kriminell, verbrecherisch**
criminal investigation	polizeiliche Ermittlung
offender [əˈfendɚ] *n*	**Straftäter(in)**
sex offender	Sexualstraftäter
offence [əˈfens] *n*	**Straftat, Vergehen**
criminal offence	strafbare Handlung

threat *n*	**Drohung**
▸ threaten sb	▸ jdn bedrohen, jdm drohen
conflict [ˈkɑːnflɪkt] *n*	**Konflikt, Auseinandersetzung**
conflict of interest	Interessenkonflikt

MAJOR THEMES AND MOTIFS 1

dispute [dɪˈspjuːt] *n*	**Streit, Streitigkeit**
commotion *n*	**Aufruhr**
assault [əˈsɔːlt] *n*	**tätlicher Angriff, Körperverletzung**
trespass [ˈtrespəs] *v*	**übertreten, widerrechtlich betreten**
ambush *n*	**Hinterhalt**

attack [əˈtæk] *n*	**Angriff**
attack sb / sth *v*	**jdn / etw angreifen**
ready to attack	angriffsbereit
defence (BE) [dɪˈfens] *n, uncount* (*defense (AE)*)	**Verteidigung**
self-defence	Selbstverteidigung
▸ defend sb / sth [dɪˈfend] *v*	▸ jdn / etw verteidigen
fight [faɪt] *n*	**Kampf, Gefecht**
get into a fight	in eine Schlägerei geraten
▸ fight (sb / sth) *v*	▸ kämpfen, sich streiten, jdn / etw bekämpfen
batter sb [ˈbætɚ] *v*	**jdn verprügeln, jdn übel zurichten**

violence [ˈvaɪələns] *n, uncount*	**Gewalt(anwendung)**
domestic violence	häusliche Gewalt
▸ violent [ˈvaɪələnt] *adj*	▸ gewalttätig, brutal
cruelty *n*	**Grausamkeit**
appalling [əˈpɔːlɪŋ] *adj*	**erschreckend, haarsträubend**

driving under the influence (DUI) *v*	**Alkohol-/Drogenmissbrauch am Steuer**
= drunk driving	Trunkenheit am Steuer
drug [drʌg] *n*	**AE: Medizin, Droge, Rauschgift**
be on drugs	auf Drogen sein
do drugs (*coll*)	Drogen nehmen
use drugs	Drogen (ein)nehmen
drug dealer	Drogendealer(in)
soft drug	weiche Droge (dessen Besitz oder Konsum in der Regel zu geringerem Strafmaß führt als bei harten Drogen)

1 MAJOR THEMES AND MOTIFS

hard drug	harte Droge (weisen psychische sowie körperliche Abhängigkeitsmerkmale auf)
drug abuse [ˈdrʌg əˌbjuːs] *n*	**Drogenmissbrauch**
drug dealer *n*	**Drogenhändler**
abuse [əˈbjuːs] *n, uncount*	**Missbrauch**
sexual abuse	sexueller Missbrauch
child abuse	Kindesmissbrauch, Kindesmisshandlung
verbal abuse	Beleidigungen
abuse sb [əˈbjuːz] *v*	**jdn missbrauchen**
kidnapper [ˈkɪdnæpə] *n*	**Entführer(in), Kidnapper(in)**
▸ kidnapping [ˈkɪdnæpɪŋ] *n*	▸ Entführung
▸ kidnap sb [ˈkɪdnæp] *v*	▸ jdn entführen, jdn kidnappen
abduct *v*	**entführen**
▸ abduction *n*	▸ Entführung
rapist [ˈreɪpɪst] *n*	**Vergewaltiger**
rape [reɪp] *n*	**Vergewaltigung**
▸ rape sb *v*	▸ jdn vergewaltigen
murder [ˈmɜːrdə] *n*	**Mord, Ermordung**
murderer [ˈmɜːrdəə] *n*	**Mörder(in)**
mass murderer	Massenmörder(in)
murder sb *v*	**jdn ermorden**
murder sb in cold blood	jdn kaltblütig ermorden
kill sb / sth [kɪl] *v*	**jdn / etw töten, umbringen**
killer [ˈkɪlə] *n*	**Mörder(in), Killer(in)**
serial killer	Serienmörder(in)
strangle sb [ˈstræŋgl] *v*	**jdn erdrosseln, jdn erwürgen**
shoot sb/ sth *v*	**erschießen, schießen**
shoot dead	erschießen

MAJOR THEMES AND MOTIFS 1

Gun ownership in the U.S.

The U.S. has the highest **gun ownership** rate in the world. Although people claim they only possess a gun to feel more secure or use it for self-defense, possessing **firearms** does not increase security. The U.S. suffers from **mass shootings** much more often than any other **developed country** – and the rate has been increasing in recent years. Unfortunately, the government has not adequately **responded to** these **developments**. Tougher **regulations** and **gun control laws** are **prohibited** by lobbyists and are not currently a priority for the Republican Party.

gun ownership *n*	Waffenbesitz
= possession of firearms	
▸ own	▸ besitzen
arms *n, pl*	Waffen
= firearms	Schusswaffen
mass shooting *n*	Massenschießerei
developed country *n*	Industriestaat
respond to a development *v*	auf eine Entwicklung reagieren
regulation *n*	Bestimmung, Vorschrift
gun control laws *n*	*Reglementierung des Waffenbesitzes*
prohibit *v*	verhindern, verbieten

---

weapon *n*	Waffe
rifle [ˈraɪfl] *n*	Gewehr
gun [gʌn] *n*	Feuerwaffe (Kanone, Gewehr, Pistole)
bullet [ˈbʊlɪt] *n*	(Gewehr-, Pistolen-)Kugel
cartridge *n*	Patrone
calibre *n*	Kaliber
lever [ˈlevɚ, ˈliːvɚ] *n*	(Lade-)Hebel
cock *v*	spannen
to cock a gun	ein Gewehr spannen, eine Waffe entsichern
aim [eɪm] *n, v*	Ziel, zielen
take aim at sb / sth	auf jdn / etw zielen
aim a gun at sb / sth	ein Gewehr auf jdn / etw richten
Don't aim that gun at me.	Ziele nicht mit dem Gewehr auf mich.

2 SETTING

> **Setting**
>
> The term '**setting**' means the **time** and **place** a literary text takes place in. At the same time, however, it refers to the **cultural, social** and **political context** the story is set in and may create a certain **atmosphere** or include the description of the (potentially **symbolic**) **scenery**.

2.1 The American South

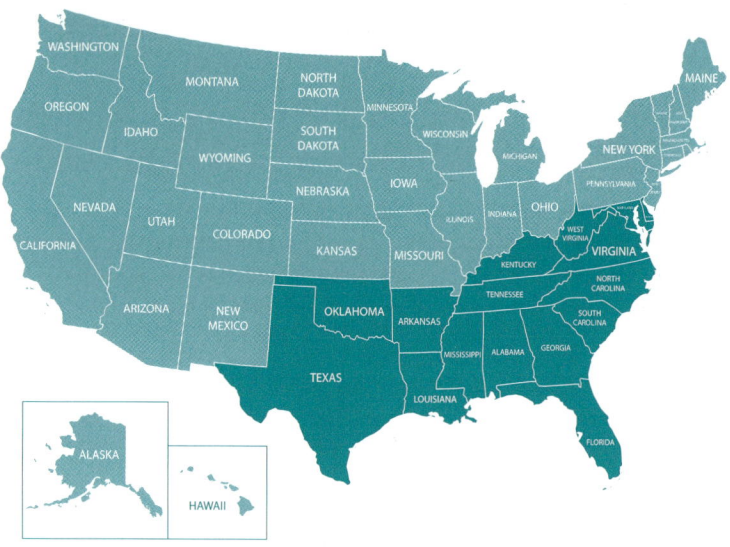

UNITED STATES OF AMERICA

SETTING 2

The American South

The term '**American South**' not only refers to the geographic south of the United States but is also used for a group of states that share a common history. They are generally defined as the states that fought for the Confederate States of America in the **American Civil War (1861-1865)**. These states (especially the '**Deep South**') relied to a huge extent on **slave labor** on their **plantations**, which involved the existence of a large African-American **population**. Unfortunately, these Southern States share a long history of racism and oppression against the African-American population.

Although agriculture was the dominant industry in the past, the area has become more industrialized and urban. Today, the American South is among the fastest-growing regions in the United States. Southerners are generally considered to be more conservative and religious than the rest of the U.S.

There are varying definitions about which states actually belong to 'the South' depending on the criteria of selection. The following states are commonly considered as Southern United States: Alabama, Arkansas (ɑːrˈkənsɑː), Florida, Georgia, Kentucky, Louisiana, Mississippi, Missouri, North Carolina, Oklahoma, South Carolina, Tennessee, Texas, Virginia, and West Virginia.

civil war *n*	Bürgerkrieg
Deep South *n*	der tiefe Süden
The Deep South is a subregion in the Southern United States. These states were commonly associated with plantations and slave societies.	
slave labor *n*	Sklavenarbeit
plantation *n*	Plantage
population *n*	Bevölkerung, Einwohnerschaft

state *n*	(Bundes-)Staat (auf Bundeslandebene)
slaveholding state *n*, *AE* ≠ non-slaveholding state	sklavenhaltender Staat
county *n* U.S. states are divided into counties.	Landkreis US-Staaten sind in Landkreise unterteilt.

2 SETTING

Mississippi

Mississippi is one of the states that belongs to the American South. Its name is derived from the Mississippi River, which flows along the western border. 'Mississippi' is the **Native American** word for 'Great River'. It has the highest percentage of African-American citizens in any U.S. state. Compared to many other states, **infrastructure** and **living conditions** are relatively bad and Mississippi is one of the poorest states in the U.S.

Native American *n*	Amerikanische(r) Ureinwohner(in)
infrastructure *n*	Infrastruktur
living conditions *n*	Lebensbedingungen
Mississippian *n*	*Einwohner Mississippis*

---

rural *adj* — ländlich
conservative [kənˈsɜːrvət̬ɪv] *adj* — konservativ
▸ conservative — ▸ Konservative(r)
backward *adj* — rückständig
unemployment *n* — Arbeitslosigkeit
 ≠ employment — ≠ Beschäftigung, Arbeit
 be unemployed — arbeitslos sein
 unemployment rate — Arbeitslosenquote
 ▸ unemployed — ▸ arbeitslos
 ▸ the unemployed — ▸ die Arbeitslosen
agribusiness *n* — Agrarindustrie
 = factory farming
timber [ˈtɪmbɚ] *n, uncount* — Bauholz
lumber industry *n* — Holzindustrie
 lumber mill — Sägemühle

2.2 Historical background

"Class systems" in the USA?

One of the USA's founding principles, once it had gained independence from Britain, was the abolition of the monarchy, of **class structures** and of the **social stratification** of the "Old Continent", Europe. **Social classes** and **hierarchies** were discarded in favor of the "self-evident truths [...] that all men are created equal, that they are endowed by their Creator with Life, Liberty and the pursuit of Happiness." (Declaration of Independence). Nevertheless, there is surely much evidence to suggest that old hierarchical **class systems** *were* very much retained, and merely replaced by a **rigid**, racially based **caste system**, with millions of cruelly enslaved African Americans firmly at its base.

class system *n*	**Klassensystem**
rigid class structure	rigide, starre Klassenstruktur
Although the class system was abolished in the USA, it was replaced by a race-based system of class.	Obwohl das Klassensystem in den USA abgeschafft wurde, wurde es durch ein rassenbasiertes Klassensystem ersetzt.
social stratification *n*	**soziale Schichtung**
hierarchy *n*	**Hierarchie**
a rigid hierarchy	eine rigide, starre Hierarchie
social hierarchy	soziale Hierarchie
social class *n*	**gesellschaftliche Schicht**
caste [kæst] *n*	**Kaste**
caste system	Kastensystem

two-class society *n*	**Zweiklassengesellschaft**
upper class [ˌʌpəˈklæs] *n*	**Oberschicht**
middle class [ˌmɪdlˈklæs] *n*	**Mittelschicht**
rich middle class	reiche Mittelschicht
lower class [ˌloʊəˈklæs] *n*	**Unterschicht**
working class [ˌwɜːrkɪŋˈklæs] *n*	**Arbeiterklasse**
poor working class	sozial schlechter gestellte Arbeiterschicht
social barrier [ˈsoʊʃəlˌberiɚ] *n*	**soziale Schranke**
social climber [ˈklaɪmɚ] *n*	**soziale(r) Aufsteiger(in)**

2 SETTING

outcast *adj*	ausgestoßen
social outcast	gesellschaftliche(r) Außenseiter(in), gesellschaftlich Augestoßene(r)
▸ outcast *n*	▸ Ausgestoßene(r)

miscegenation [ˌmɪsɪdʒɪˈneɪʃᵊn] *n*	interkulturelle Ehe, Rassenmischung
white supremacy *n* *(racist terminology)*	Vorherrschaft der Weißen
white trash *n (derog)*	weißes Pack, weißer Abschaum
xenophobia [ˌzenəˈfoʊbiə] *n, no pl* *(fear or dislike of people from other countries)*	Fremdenhass, Xenophobie
racism [ˈreɪsɪzᵊm] *n, uncount*	Rassismus
▸ racist	▸ Rasist, rassistisch

race *n*	Rasse
race conflict *n* = racial conflict	Rassenkonflikt
race hatred, racial hatred *n*	Rassenhass
racial prejudice *n*	Vorurteile gegen andere Rassen
▸ prejudiced	▸ voreingenommen
biased [ˈbaɪəst] *adj*	voreingenommen
be heavily biased	sehr voreingenommen sein
minority [maɪˈnɔːrəti] *n*	Minderheit
an ethnic minority	eine ethnische Minderheit
pejorative [pɪˈdʒɔːrətɪv] *adj*	herabsetzend, pejorativ
insult [ˈɪnsʌlt] *n*	Beleidigung
▸ insult (sb) [ɪnˈsʌlt] *v*	▸ (jdn) beleidigen
▸ insulting [ɪnˈsʌltɪŋ] *adj*	▸ beleidigend, schmähend
▸ insultingly *adv*	▸ beleidigend, in beleidigender Weise
offensive *adj* = objectionable	anstößig, beleidigend
humiliation [hjuːˌmɪliˈeɪʃᵊn] *n*	Beschämung, Demütigung, Erniedrigung
▸ humiliate sb	▸ jdn demütigen, erniedrigen

SETTING 2

Jim Crow and the "separate but equal" doctrine

"Jim Crow" is an African American character in a 19th-century **minstrel song**. This character represents a viciously stereotyped, racist image of African Americans. The term "Jim Crow Laws" refers to the system of **racial segregation** and oppression established in the U.S. after the Civil War. The **doctrine** "separate but equal" came to summarize the concept of Jim Crow and segregation and was **affirmed** by the U.S. **Supreme Court** in 1896. According to the Jim Crow Laws, whites and African Americans were to have **distinctly separate** spheres, e.g. separate schools, separate water fountains, separate entrances to buildings, separate seating in public transportation and buildings. It was only in 1954 that the **Supreme Court overturned** the segregation of schools. It would take another ten years, until 1964, when the "separate but equal" doctrine was **revoked** by the Civil Rights Act and racial segregation was officially ended.

minstrel song *n*	Variétélied, von einem als Afro-Amerikaner verkleideten („blackface") Sänger vorgetragen *(In den Aufführungen wurden Schwarze karikiert und vorgeführt sowie rassistische Stereotypen perpetuiert.)*
segregate [ˈsegrəgeɪt] *v*	trennen
(racial) segregation [ˌsegrəˈgeɪʃ°n] *n*	Rassentrennung
doctrine [ˈdɑːktrɪn] *n*	Doktrin, Grundsatz
teach a doctrine	eine Lehre verbreiten
affirm *v*	bestätigen
Supreme Court *n*	Oberster Gerichtshof
separation [ˌsepərˈeɪʃ°n] *n, uncount*	Trennung, Teilung
separation of powers	Gewaltenteilung
separation of church and state	Trennung von Kirche und Staat
distinctly *adv*	klar, deutlich
overturn *v*	umkippen, stürzen
overturn a verdict	ein Urteil aufheben
revoke *v*	rückgängig machen, aufheben

2 SETTING

African Americans as alleged rapists

There was one particularly powerful racist stereotype: that of the **oversexed beast**. This myth suggested that all African-American males were **lecherous savages**, driven solely by their **sex drive**. Allegedly, they **lusted** particularly after white women, stalked and frequently raped them. If an African-American man was accused of assaulting a white woman, he was doomed: more often than not, he would be **lynched**. A prominent example is the case of **Emmet Till** in 1955. He was an African-American teenager from Chicago who was lynched in Mississippi at the age of 14 after reportedly flirting with a white woman. His killers were acquitted, **triggering a public outcry**.

In *Crooked Letter, Crooked Letter* this stereotype is also present, e.g. when Cindy is asked by a white man whether Silas is bothering her (p. 244, l. 11)) or when Alice warns her son not to see a white girl and reminds him of Emmet Till (p. 246, l. 27 f). There is a parallel drawn between Silas and Emmet Till, who both come from Chicago in the north to the American South. In the book, the stereotype seems to be reversed, though, when Larry Ott (a white man) is accused of rape.

oversexed *adj*	sexbesessen
beast *n*	wildes Tier
lecherous [ˈletʃərəs] *adj*	lüstern
savage *adj*	unzivilisiert, wild
▸ savage *n*	▸ der, die Wilde
sex drive *n*	Sexualtrieb
lust after (sb/sth) *v*	(jdn / etw) begehren
trigger a public outcry *v*	eine öffentliche Protestwelle verursachen
lynch [lɪn(t)ʃ] *v*	jdn lynchen
= murder, kill	= umbringen, töten
▸ lynching [ˈlɪn(t)ʃɪŋ] *n*	▸ Lynchmord

oppression *n*	Unterdrückung
discrimination (against) *n*	Diskriminierung (von)
persecution *n*	Verfolgung
▸ to persecute sb	▸ jdn verfolgen
suffering *n*	Leiden
mob *n*	Mob, Pöbel
lynch mob	Lynchmob

SETTING 2

The African-American Civil Rights Movement

The African-American **Civil Rights Movement** refers to the social movements in the United States aimed at **outlawing** racial discrimination against black Americans and restoring **voting rights** to them. It was mainly characterized by **non-violent protests**, including **boycotts, sit-ins** and **mass demonstrations,** in the South during the **1950s and 1960s**. A prominent leader of the movement was Martin Luther King, Jr. (1929-68). The emergence of the **Black Power Movement**, which lasted roughly from **1966 to 1975**, expanded the aims of the Civil Rights Movement to include racial **dignity**, economic and political **self-sufficiency**, and freedom from oppression by white Americans. The movement grew more and more radical and did not **hesitate** to use violence in order to achieve its aims. The term **'freedom struggle'** is now preferably used when referring to the ongoing struggle of African-Americans for freedom, **equality**, and full **citizenship** in a racist society.

Civil Rights Movement n	Bürgerrechtsbewegung (die sich in den USA von 1954-68 für die Gleichberechtigung von Schwarzen einsetzte)
civil rights [ˌsɪvəlˈraɪts] n, pl	Bürgerrechte
outlaw sth v	etw für ungesetzlich erklären
right to vote n	Wahlrecht
universal suffrage [ˈsʌfrɪdʒ] n	allgemeines Wahlrecht
non-violence n	Gewaltlosigkeit
Martin Luther King was committed to non-violence.	Martin Luther King setzte sich für Gewaltlosigkeit ein.
boycott n	Boykott
The Montgomery bus boycott was started in 1955 by Rosa Parks.	Der Busboykott von Montgomery wurde 1955 durch Rosa Parks ausgelöst.
sit-in n	Sitzstreik
mass demonstration n	Massendemonstration
dignity n	Würde
self-sufficiency n	Selbstversorgung, Eigenständigkeit
hesitate v	zögern
equality n	Gleichheit, Gleichberechtigung
≠ inequality	≠ Ungleichheit
citizenship n	Staatsbürgerschaft

2 SETTING

School integration in the United States

One of the key aims of the Civil Rights Movement was the **desegregation of schools**. Although segregation was supposed to follow the policy of **'separate but equal'**, **facilities** for black people were far worse than the facilities for whites, which was particularly striking in the field of education. Quality education was seen as the key for a better future, especially for the African-American population. In 1954, the **United States Supreme Court** concluded that separate schools for black and white students were **unconstitutional**. However, the decision faced massive **resistance** and it took a long time until schools were actually integrated.

desegregation n	Aufhebung der Rassentrennung
= integration	
facility n	Einrichtung, Anlage
United States Supreme Court n	Oberster Gerichtshof der Vereinigten Staaten
unconstitutional adj	verfassungswidrig
resistance [rɪˈzɪstəns] n, uncount	Widerstand
passive resistance	passiver Widerstand

Politically correct terminology

Please note: It is of great importance that politically correct, non-racist terms are used!

The politically correct, acceptable terms when discussing *Crooked Letter, Crooked Letter* or any aspect of race and/or African-American culture, history etc. are either **"African American"** (both as an adjective and noun; the adjective is usually written *with* a hyphen, the noun *not*), or **"black"**. The terms "nigger" and "negro" are racist, very offensive, insulting and derogatory and should not be used under any circumstances! These terms may only be used when quoting from the text. The term "colored" is also to be avoided because it is often associated with segregation laws in the U.S. and terminology in apartheid South Africa, and is thus often considered racist today.

awareness n	Bewusstsein, Wahrnehmung
growing awareness of sth	zunehmende Wahrnehmung einer Sache
historical awareness n	Geschichtsbewusstsein

SETTING 2

collective memory *n*
Catastrophes in history, such as the Holocaust and the World Wars, remain in the collective memory of the people who suffered through them.

whitewash *v*
Hollywood is whitewashing a majority of its movies.

concern [kənˈsɜːrn] *n*
aftermath *n (the period of time after a bad and usually destructive event)*
legacy *n*

kollektives Gedächtnis
Geschichtliche Katastrophen, z. B. der Holocaust und die Weltkriege, bleiben im kollektiven Gedächtnis der Völker, die sie durchlitten haben, erhalten.

weißwaschen
In Hollywood werden viele Filme weiß gewaschen (es gibt nur weiße Hauptdarsteller etc.).

Bedenken, Sorge
Folgen, Nachwirkungen

Vermächtnis, Erbe

Affirmative action

Affirmative action in the United States refers to public **policies** that were developed in order to address long histories of discrimination faced by minorities and women. These measures are a subject of **controversy** in American politics and raise legal, political, and ethnical questions of equality and fairness. The debate revolves around **preferential treatment**, **compensation** for past injustice, **reverse discrimination** as well as ethnic and gender **diversity**.

affirmative action *n (law)*	**aktive Förderungsmaßnahmen zu Gunsten von Minderheiten**
policy *n*	**Politik, Grundsatz, Richtlinie**
controversy *n*	**Auseinandersetzungen, Kontroverse**
preferential treatment [ˌprefᵊrˈen(t)ʃᵊl] *n*	**Vorzugsbehandlung**
compensation *n*	**Entschädigung, Schadenersatz**
(reverse) discrimination *n*	**(umgekehrte) Diskriminierung**
diversity *n*	**Vielfalt**

2 SETTING

2.3 Surroundings

2.3.1 Mood and ambience

decay *n*	Verfall, Niedergang
hidden *adj*	versteckt
secluded *adj*	abgelegen, einsam
deserted *adj*	einsam, verlassen
abandoned *adj*	verlassen
vacant *adj*	frei, leerstehend
pristine *adj*	unberührt
exposed [ɪkˈspoʊzd] *adj*	ausgesetzt, exponiert
exposed to rain, wind	dem Regen, Wind ausgesetzt sein

dubious [ˈduːbiəs] *adj*	dubios, fragwürdig, zweifelhaft
perilous *adj*	bedrohlich
frightening *adj*	furchterregend, beängstigend
creepy *adj*	gruselig
mysterious *adj*	geheimnisvoll
gloomy *adj*	bedrückend
dim *adj*	schummrig
haunted places *n*	Orte, an denen es spuken soll, verwunschene Orte

muggy *adj*	schwül
clammy *adj*	klamm
moldy *adj (BE* mouldy*)*	modrig
foul *adj*	übelriechend
humid (air) *adj*	feucht(e Luft)
odor *n*	Geruch
whiff *n*	Hauch

2.3.2 Housing

veranda *n*	**Veranda**
porch [pɔːrtʃ] *n*	*BE:* **Vorbau, Vordach;** *AE:* **Veranda**
wooden porch	Holzveranda
attic [ˈæt̬ɪk] *n*	**Dachboden**
deck *n*	**Sonnenterrasse**
drive *n*	**Einfahrt**
closet [ˈklɑːzɪt] *n, AE*	**Wandschrank, Kleiderschrank**
= cabinet	Schrank, Vitrine
faucet [ˈfɑːsɪt] *n, AE ((water) tap (BE))*	**Wasserhahn**

barn *n*	**Scheune**
shack *n*	**Verschlag**
cabin [ˈkæbɪn] *n*	**kleines Holzhaus (im Wald/ Gebirge), Hütte**
hut *n*	**Hütte**
litter *n, sing*	**Abfall**
= waste / rubbish	

2.3.3 Flora and fauna

wilderness *n*	**Wildnis**
lush *adj*	**üppig**
creek *n*	**Bach**
swamp *n*	**Sumpf(gebiet)**
puddle *n*	**Pfütze**
(common) reed *n (bot.)*	**Schilf(gras)**
cattail *n (bot.)*	**Lampenputzer**
underbrush *n*	**Unterholz**
foliage [ˈfoʊliɪdʒ] *n*	**Laub**
fern *n*	**Farn**
kudzu *n*	**Kudzu, Kopoubohne**

2 SETTING

> ### Kudzu
> Kudzu is a very typical plant in the American South. It is a fast growing vine that was imported from Japan. It grows so rapidly and vigorously that it sometimes covers trees, empty houses, telegraph poles or even cars.

loblolly pine *n*	Weihrauchkiefer
crop [krɑːp] *n*	Feldfrucht, Ernte
ripe crop	reife Frucht
= harvest *n*, *v*	Ernte, ernten

reptiles *n*	Reptilien
snake [sneɪk] *n*	Schlange
cottonmouth *n*	Wassermokkasin (Schlange)
rattlesnake *n*	Klapperschlange
lizard [ˈlɪzɚd] *n*	Eidechse
dangerous [ˈdeɪndʒərəs] *adj*	gefährlich
≠ harmless	≠ ungefährlich, harmlos
venomous *adj*	giftig
= poisonous	
venomous snake	Giftschlange

pitbull *n*	Pitbull
mongrel *n* *(derog)*	Mischling
squirrel [ˈskwɜrəl] *n*	Eichhörnchen
buzzard [ˈbʌzɚd] *n*	Bussard
gnat [næt] *n*	Mücke
bullfrog *n*	Ochsenfrosch
catfish *n*	Wels

chicken [ˈtʃɪkɪn] *n*	Huhn
a chicken clucks	ein Huhn gackert
hen [hen] *n*	Henne, Huhn
hens lay eggs	Hühner legen Eier
rooster *n*	Hahn
chicken coop *n*	Hühnerstall

SETTING 2

2.4 Occupations and workplaces

2.4.1 Police

police *n*	Polizei
police officer [pəˈliːsˌɑːfɪsɚ] *n*	Polizeibeamter, Polizeibeamtin
cop *n (coll)*	Bulle, Cop
police station [pəˈliːsˌsteɪʃ°n] *n*	Polizeiwache
crime scene *n*	Tatort
town hall [ˌtaʊnˈhɔːl] *n*	Rathaus
law enforcement *n*	Gesetzesvollzug
investigation [ɪnˌvestɪˈgeɪʃ°n] *n*	Untersuchung, Ermittlung
ongoing investigation	laufende Ermittlung
observation [ˌɑːbzɚˈveɪʃ°n] *n*	Beobachtung
under observation	unter Beobachtung

...

suspect [ˈsʌspekt] *n*	Verdächtige(r)
prime (or main) suspect	Hauptverdächtige(r)
▸ suspect [ˈsʌspekt]	▸ verdächtig, suspekt
▸ suspect sb of doing sth [səˈspekt]	▸ jdn verdächtigen, etw getan zu haben
hunch *n*	Ahnung
pursue sth [pɚˈsuː] *v*	einer Sache nachgehen
hunt [hʌnt] *v; n*	jagen, auf die Jagd gehen; Jagd
lead [liːd] *n*	heiße Spur
dissolve *v*	auflösen
curb sth [kɜːrb] *v*	etw bremsen, beeinträchtigen
delay sth *v*	etw verschieben; etw verzögern

...

apprehend *v*	festnehmen
handcuffs *n, pl*	Handschellen
wrist [rɪst] *n*	Handgelenk
glove [glʌv] *n*	Handschuh
a pair of gloves	ein Paar Handschuhe
tweezers *n, pl*	Pinzette
coroner [ˈkɔːrəʳnɚ] *n*	Gerichtsmediziner
crime scene technician *n*	Kriminaltechniker(in)

2 SETTING

2.4.2 Ottomotive Repair

garage AE [gəˈrɑːʒ] n	(Auto)Werkstatt
car mechanic n	Automechaniker(in)
screwdriver [ˈskruːdraɪvɚ] n	Schraubenzieher
wrench [rentʃ] n, AE	Schraubenschlüssel

exhaust (tailpipe) n	Auspuff
high beams n	Fernlicht
ignition [ɪgˈnɪʃən] n	Zündung
clutch [klʌtʃ] n	Kupplung
operate the clutch	kuppeln
let the clutch out	die Kupplung kommen lassen
odometer n	Kilometerzähler
car exhausts [ˌkɑːrˈɪgzɔːsts] n, pl	Autoabgase
convertible [kənˈvɜːrtəbl] n	Cabrio(let)
SUV (sport utility vehicle) [ˌesjuːˈviː] n	Geländewagen, SUV
accelerate v	beschleunigen
reverse v	zurücksetzen, umkehren

2.4.3 Hospital

hospital [ˈhɑːspɪtəl] n	Krankenhaus
take sb to hospital	jdn ins Krankenhaus einliefern
▸ be admitted to hospital	▸ ins Krankenhaus eingeliefert werden
	Bei stationären Patienten im BE ohne 'the': She's in hospital. Bei Besuchern, Angestellten oder ambulanten Patienten mit 'the': I have to go to the hospital for my regular check-up today. / She works at the hospital.
ward [wɔːrd] n	Krankenstation (im Krankenhaus)
children's ward	Kinderstation
psychiatric ward	psychiatrische Abteilung

SETTING 2

ICU [ˌaɪsiːˈjuː] *n (intensive care unit)*	**Intensivstation**
be in (the) ICU	auf der Intensivstation liegen
nurse [nɜːrs] *n*	**Krankenschwester**
surgeon [ˈsɜːrdʒᵊn] *n*	**Chirurg(in)**
emergency service *n*	**Notfalldienst, Notdienst**

life support *n*	**lebenserhaltende Maßnahmen**
breathing support	Atmungsunterstützung, Beatmung
injection *n*	**Injektion, Spritze**
drip *n*	**Tropf**
= intravenous (IV)	intravenös
be on a drip	am Tropf hängen, eine Infusion bekommen

crutch *n*	**Krücke**
gash *n*	**Schnittwunde**
chapped *adj*	**rissig**
hoarse *adj*	**heiser**

unconscious *adj*	**bewusstlos**
≠ conscious	≠ bewusst, wach
drift in and out of consciousness	abwechselnd zu Bewusstsein kommen und wieder bewusstlos werden
regain consciousness	das Bewusstsein wiedererlangen, zu sich kommen
dizziness [ˈdɪzɪnəs] *n*	**Schwindelgefühl**
drowsy *adj*	**schwindelig, schläfrig, benommen**
numb *adj*	**taub**

inhale *v*	**einatmen**
≠ exhale	≠ ausatmen
recovery *n*	**Genesung, Erholung**
▸ recover from sth	▸ sich von etw erholen

2 SETTING

health *n* — Gesundheit
  be in good health — bei guter Gesundheit sein
  physical and mental health — körperliche und geistige Gesundheit
  health disorders — gesundheitliche Probleme

2.4.4 Journalism

journalism [ˈdʒɜːrnəlɪzəm] *n* — **Journalismus**
journalist [ˈdʒɜːrnəlɪst] *n* — **Journalist(in)**
  sports journalist — Sportjournalist(in)
reporter *n* — **Reporter(in)**
  on-the-scene reporter — Vor-Ort-Reporter(in)
newspaper [ˈnuːzˌpeɪpɚ] *n* — **Zeitung**
  = paper [ˈpeɪpə]
  local newspaper — Lokalblatt, Lokalzeitung
  daily newspaper — Tageszeitung
  quality newspaper — seriöse Zeitung
weekly (newspaper) [ˈwiːkli] *n* — **Wochenzeitung**
front cover *n* — **Titelseite**
headline [ˈhedlaɪn] *n* — **Schlagzeile**
  newspaper headline — Zeitungsschlagzeile
  news headlines (pl) — (Nachrichten-)Schlagzeilen
  make headlines — Schlagzeilen machen

objective *adj* — **objektiv, sachlich**
  ≠ subjective — ≠ subjektiv
  stay objective — objektiv bleiben
sensationalism [senˈseɪʃənəlɪzəm] *n* — **Sensationsgier, Effekthascherei**
influence (on sb / sth) [ˈɪnfluəns] *n* — **Einfluss (auf jdn / etw)**
  a powerful influence — ein starker Einfluss
  have an influence on sb / sth — Einfluss auf jdn / etw haben

CHARACTERIZATION 3

3.1 General terms

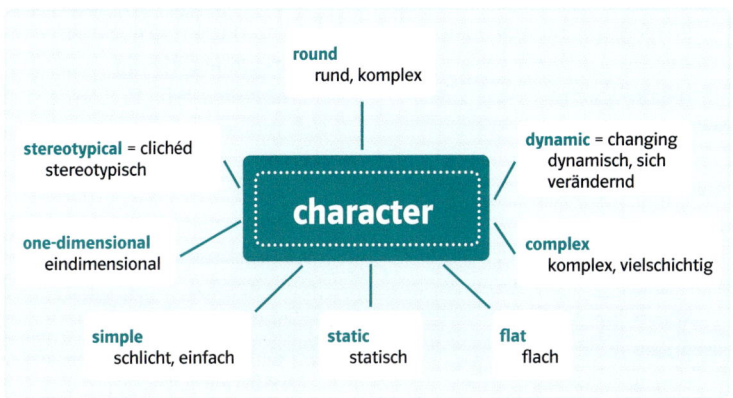

characterization [ˌkerəktərˈzeɪʃᵊn] *n*	**Charakterisierung, Personenbeschreibung**
characterization by the narrator	Charakterisierung durch den Erzähler
characterization by another character	Charakterisierung durch einen anderen Charakter
self-characterization	Selbstcharakterisierung
explicit *adj*	**ausdrücklich, deutlich, explizit**
≠ implicit	≠ indirekt
explicit and implicit characterization	direkte und indirekte Charakterisierung
character [ˈkerəktɚ] *n (in Erzählungen bzw. Dramen)*	**Figur, Person, Rolle**
main character	Hauptperson
minor character	Nebenfigur
protagonist [proʊˈtægᵊnɪst] *n*	**Hauptfigur**
≠ antagonist	≠ Gegenspieler(in)
hero(ine) [ˈhɪroʊ, ˈheroʊɪn] *n*	**Held(in)**
≠ anti-hero	≠ Antiheld(in)
feature *n*	**Merkmal, Charakteristikum**
(character) trait [treɪt] *n*	**Eigenschaft, Charakterzug**

3 CHARACTERIZATION

character constellation n	Figurenkonstellation
= relationships between the characters	
character development n	Charakterentwicklung
develop v	sich entwickeln
change v	sich verändern
grow up v	aufwachsen
mature v	reifen
▸ maturation	▸ Heranreifen, Reifung
▸ maturity	▸ Erwachsensein, Reife

---

gender [ˈdʒendə] n	Geschlecht
ethnicity [eθˈnɪsəti] n	Ethnie, Volkszugehörigkeit, Ethnizität
appearance [əˈpɪərəns] n, uncount	Aussehen, Erscheinung
outward appearance	äußeres Erscheinungsbild, Aussehen
posture [ˈpɑːstʃə] n	Körperhaltung
profession [prəˈfeʃən] n	Beruf *(der eine besondere Ausbildung bzw. besondere Qualifikationen voraussetzt)*
the medical profession	die Ärzteschaft, der Arztberuf
by profession	von Beruf
practical skills n, pl	praktische Fertigkeiten
origin [ˈɔːrədʒɪn] n	Ursprung, Herkunft
of Native American origin	(ur)amerikanischer Herkunft
place of residence [pleɪsəvˈrezɪdəns] n	Wohnort
marital status [ˌmerɪtʃəlˈstætəs] n	Familienstand
social status n	soziale Position
financial status n	finanzielle Situation

---

norms and values n	Normen und Werte
(psychological) disposition n	Gemüt, Veranlagung, Disposition
attitude n	Einstellung, Haltung
attitude towards life	Lebenseinstellung
self-esteem n	Selbstbewusstsein
He sure has a high self-esteem.	Er ist sehr selbstbewusst.
After these people had bullied her, her self-esteem was really low.	Nachdem diese Leute sie so gemobbt hatten, war ihr Selbstbewusstsein sehr niedrig.

CHARACTERIZATION 3

mood *n* — Stimmung, Laune
  in a good, bad mood — gut, schlecht gelaunt
  celebratory mood — Feierlaune
  mood-lifting — stimmungshebend
  ▸ moody — ▸ launisch, sprunghaft
temper *n* — Laune, Wut
  lose one's temper — wütend werden, die Geduld verlieren
  have quite a temper — leicht reizbar sein
  be in a (bad) temper — schlecht gelaunt sein, gereizt sein
knowledge *n* — Wissen, Kenntnis
  level of knowledge — Wissensstand
reputation *n* — Ansehen, Ruf
  good, bad reputation — guter, schlechter Ruf

---

experience (disappointments) *v* — **(Enttäuschungen) erfahren**
make decisions *v* — **Entscheidungen treffen**
face (conflicts) *v* — **sich (Konflikten) stellen**
solve (problems) *v* — **(Probleme) lösen**
enter into a relationship *v* — **eine Beziehung eingehen**
reappraise the past *v* — **die Vergangenheit aufarbeiten**
  = come to terms with the past
make up for sth *v* — **etw wiedergutmachen**
  = make amends

3.2 Main characters

3.2.1 Larry Ott

As a child

pudgy *adj (coll)* — **pummelig**
olive (skin) *adj* — **olivenfarbene Haut**
soft [sɑːft] *adj* — **weich, zart**
weak [wiːk] *adj* — **schwach, geschwächt**
  ≠ strong
feminine [ˈfemɪnɪn] *adj* — **weiblich, Frauen-**

3 CHARACTERIZATION

glasses [ˈglæsəz] *n, pl*	Brille
wear glasses	eine Brille tragen
stutter *v*	stottern
asthma *n*	Asthma
allergy [ˈælədʒi] *n*	Allergie
allergy sufferers	Allergiker(innen)

curious [ˈkjʊriəs] *adj*	neugierig
sneaky *adj*	gewieft, raffiniert
passive [ˈpæsɪv] *adj*	passiv, untätig
momma's boy *n (coll)*	Muttersöhnchen
clumsy *adj*	ungeschickt
shy *adj*	schüchtern
go hunting *v*	auf die Jagd gehen
fishing *n*	Fischfang
bookworm *n*	Bücherwurm
horror [ˈhɔːrɚ] *n*	Horror

be bullied (at school) *v*	(in der Schule) gemobbt werden
be included in *v*	dazugehören
= be part of	
fit in *v*	sich einfügen, dazugehören
fit in with a team	sich in ein Team einfügen
recognition [ˌrekəgˈnɪʃ°n] *n*	Anerkennung
gain recognition	Anerkennung finden
unworthiness *n*	Unwürdigkeit

As an adult

lean *adj*	schlank
= slim	
unkempt *adj*	ungepflegt
clean shaven *adj*	glattrasiert
neat and tidy *adj*	sauber und ordentlich

CHARACTERIZATION 3

single *adj*	ledig, unverheiratet, single
virgin *n*	Jungfrau
well-read *adj*	belesen
well-educated *adj*	gebildet
open-minded *adj*	vorurteilslos
Methodist *n*	Methodist *(relig. Strömung)*
abstinent *adj*	enthaltsam (Alkoholgegner)
passive ['pæsɪv] *adj*	passiv, untätig

insecure *adj*	unsicher
sad [sæd] *adj*	traurig
lonely ['loʊnli] *adj*	einsam
resigned *adj*	resigniert
naive *adj*	naiv
gullible *adj*	leichtgläubig
▸ gullibility	▸ Leichtgläubigkeit

hopeful *adj*	hoffnungsvoll, zuversichtlich
dutiful *adj*	pflichtbewusst
caring *adj*	fürsorglich
attentive *adj*	aufmerksam
kind [kaɪnd] *adj*	liebenswürdig, freundlich
▸ kindness	▸ Liebenswürdigkeit, Freundlichkeit
good-natured *adj* = good-humoured	gut gelaunt, gutmütig
patient *adj, uncount*	geduldig
▸ patience ['peɪʃ°ns]	▸ Geduld
sympathetic [ˌsɪmpə'θeṯɪk] *adj*	mitfühlend, verständnisvoll
▸ sympathy for sb ['sɪmpəθi]	▸ Mitleid, Mitgefühl mit jdm
handy ['hændi] *adj, FF*	praktisch, nützlich, geschickt
≠ clumsy	≠ ungeschickt
clever ['klevɚ] *adj*	klug, schlau
be clever at sth	geschickt in etw sein

3 CHARACTERIZATION

army [ˈɑːrmi] *n*	**Armee**
military [ˈmɪlɪteri] *adj*	**militärisch, Militär-**
habit [ˈhæbɪt] *n (regular activity)*	**Gewohnheit**
set in one's ways *adj*	**in eigenen Gewohnheiten festgefahren**
accomplished *adj*	**versiert**
caretaker [ˈkerˌteɪkɚ] *n*	**Hausmeister**
sustain *v*	**aufrechterhalten**
car mechanic *n*	**Automechaniker(in)**
inventiveness *n*	**Erfindungsgabe, Einfallsreichtum**

---

reputation *n*	**Ansehen, Ruf**
good, bad reputation	guter, schlechter Ruf
famous [ˈfeɪməs] *adj*	**berühmt**
≠ infamous [ˈɪnfəməs]	≠ verrufen, berüchtigt
solitary *adj*	**einsam**
be the object of criticism and ridicule *v*	**Zielscheibe der Kritik und des Gespötts sein**
exclude sb from sth [ɪksˈkluːd] *v*	**jdn von etw ausschließen**
excluded from society	von der Gesellschaft ausgeschlossen
marginalize sb [ˈmɑːrdʒɪnəlaɪz] *v*	**jdn an den Rand drängen, jdn marginalisieren**
be ostracized *v*	**ausgeschlossen / ausgegrenzt werden**

---

odd [ɑːd] *adj*	**sonderbar, eigenartig**
the odd one out	das fünfte Rad am Wagen, Außenseiter
He was always the odd one out at school.	Er war immer der Außenseiter in der Schule.
psycho [ˈsaɪkoʊ] *n (derog, coll)*	**Verrückte(r), Psychopath(in)**
outcast [ˈaʊtkæst] *n*	**Außenseiter(in), Ausgestoßene(r)**
a social outcast	ein gesellschaftlicher Außenseiter
unrespected *adj*	**unangesehen**
disapprove [ˌdɪsəˈpruːv] *v*	**schlecht finden, missbilligen**
invisible *adj*	**unsichtbar**
boring [ˈbɔːrɪŋ] *adj*	**langweilig**

CHARACTERIZATION 3

3.2.2 Silas Jones

As a child

poverty [ˈpɑːvəti] *n*	Armut
≠ wealth	
▸ poor	▸ arm
single mother *n*	alleinerziehende Mutter
impediment *n*	Hindernis
insurmountable impediment	unüberwindliches Hindernis
African-American /	Afro-Amerikaner(in), Schwarz-
Black American *n; adj*	Amerikaner(in); afro-amerikanisch

---

alert [əˈlɜːrt] *adj*	aufmerksam
brave *adj*	mutig, tapfer
self-confident [ˌselfˈkɑːnfədənt] *adj*	selbstbewusst, selbstsicher
be fortunate *v*	glücklich sein, Glück haben
popular [ˈpɑːpjələr] *adj*	beliebt, gefragt
popular with	beliebt bei
athletic *adj*	sportlich, athletisch
baseball [ˈbeɪsbɔːl] *n, uncount*	Baseball
baseball bat	Baseballschläger
practice [ˈpræktɪs] *n*	Training
sports scholarship *n*	Sportstipendium
professional [prəˈfeʃənəl] *adj; n*	Profi-, Berufs-; Profi
professional athlete	Berufssportler(in)

---

foolishness *n*	Dummheit
inner conflict *n*	Zerrissenheit
screw up *v (coll)*	versagen, versemmeln
unfaithful *adj*	untreu
≠ faithful	
disloyal *adj*	illoyal
≠ loyal	
irresponsible *adj*	verantwortungslos
egoistic, egotistic *adj*	egoistisch
= selfish	

3 CHARACTERIZATION

betrayal n	Verrat
▸ betrayed	▸ verraten, betrogen

As an adult

attractive [əˈtræktɪv] adj	attraktiv, anziehend
sexually attractive	sexuell attraktiv
ladies' man n	Frauenheld
active [ˈæktɪv] adj	aktiv, beweglich
atheist [ˈeɪθiːɪst] n	Atheist(in)
evasive adj	ausweichend
vague [veɪg] adj	vage, undeutlich, nebelhaft
nickname [ˈnɪkneɪm] n	Spitzname
traffic warden [ˈtræfɪkˌwɔːrdᵊn] n	Verkehrspolizist *(aber auch:)* Hilfspolizist, Politesse
constable n	Polizist
owe sb sth v	jdm etw schulden, schuldig sein
You owe me an explanation.	Du bist mir eine Erklärung schuldig.
responsible [rɪˈspɑːnsəbl] adj	verantwortungsbewusst; verantwortlich
feel responsible for sb	sich für jdn verantwortlich fühlen
hold sb responsible for sth	jdn für etw verantwortlich machen
empathy n	Einfühlungsvermögen, Empathie
feel empathy for	sich hineinversetzen in
▸ empathize *(with sb)*	▸ sich (in jdn) hineinfühlen
blame [bleɪm] n	Schuld
lay the blame on sb	jdm die Schuld zuschieben
reject the blame	die Schuld von sich weisen
share the blame	eine Mitschuld tragen
be to blame (for sth)	Schuld (an etw) haben
guilt n	Schuld
▸ guilty	▸ schuldig, schuldbewusst

CHARACTERIZATION 3

conscience [ˈkɑːn(t)ʃ°n(t)s] *n* — **Gewissen**
  bad conscience — schlechtes Gewissen
  in good conscience — guten Gewissens
conscience-stricken *adj* — **schuldbewusst**
remorse *n* — **Reue, Schuldgefühle**
penance *n* — **Buße**
  = atonement
redemption *n* — **Wiedergutmachung**
  ▸ redeem oneself — ▸ sich reinwaschen, sich rehabilitieren

3.2.3 Wallace Stringfellow

stringy *adj* — **sehnig**
skinny *adj* — **dünn**
  = lean — schlank
scruffy *adj* — **verwahrlost**
  = disheveled *AE* — ungepflegt
dirty [ˈdɜːrt̬i] *adj* — **schmutzig**
ratty *adj* — **schäbig**

slick *adj* — **glatt, raffiniert**
unscrupulous *adj* — **skrupellos**
  ▸ scruple — ▸ Skrupel
disrespectful *adj* — **respektlos**
uneducated *adj* — **ungebildet**
  ≠ educated — ≠ gebildet
intrusive *adj* — **aufdringlich**
dodgy *adj (coll)* — **zwielichtig**
creepy *adj* — **gruselig, unheimlich, schmierig**
strange *adj* — **seltsam**
mentally ill *adj* — **psychisch krank**
psychopath — **psychisch kranker Mensch**

stalker *n* — **Stalker(in)**
addict [ˈædɪkt] *n* — **Abhängige(r), Süchtige(r)**
  a drug addict — ein Drogensüchtiger
psychotic [saɪˈkɑːt̬ɪk] *n, adj* — **Psychotiker(in), psychotisch**

3 CHARACTERIZATION

rapist *n*	Vergewaltiger
criminal [ˈkrɪmɪnəl] *adj; n*	kriminell, verbrecherisch; Verbrecher(in)
a criminal act	Straftat, kriminelle Handlung
killer [ˈkɪlɚ] *n*	Mörder, Killer
racist *n*	Rassist(in)
coward [ˈkaʊɚd] *n*	Feigling
▸ cowardice [ˈkaʊɚdɪs]	▸ Feigheit
▸ cowardly	▸ feige
liar *n*	Lügner(in)
hillbilly *n (derog)*	Hinterwäldler
homophobia [ˌhoʊməˈfoʊbiə] *n, no pl*	Homophobie
▸ homophobic	▸ homophob

disguise *v*	maskieren, tarnen, verkleiden
disguise oneself (as sb, sth)	sich (als etw, jmd) verkleiden
fascinated *adj*	begeistert
revenge *n*	Rache
▸ revenge (sth)	▸ (etw) rächen
bully sb *v*	jmd drangsalieren, mobben
mess with *v*	anlegen mit, sich einmischen; spielen mit, hintergehen, verspotten

betray *v*	verraten, betrügen
loiter *v*	herumlungern
terrarium *n*	Terrarium
(place where you'd keep pet snakes/reptiles e.g.)	

3.3 Side characters

3.3.1 Cindy Walker

blond(e) [blɑːnd] *adj*	blond
freckles *n*	Sommersprossen
pretty [ˈprɪti] *adj*	hübsch

CHARACTERIZATION 3

ambitious [æmˈbɪʃəs] *adj*	**ehrgeizig, anspruchsvoll**
brave [breɪv] *adj*	**mutig, tapfer**
= courageous	
desperate *adj*	**verzweifelt**
▸ despair	▸ Verzweiflung
pregnant [ˈpregnənt] *adj*	**schwanger**
get pregnant	schwanger werden
be pregnant (by sb)	(von jdm) schwanger sein
get sb pregnant	jdn schwängern
be X months pregnant	im X. Monat schwanger sein
secret *adj*	**geheim**
exploit sb [ɪkˈsplɔɪt] *v*	**jmdn ausnutzen, ausbeuten**
mixed-race relationship *n*	**Beziehung zwischen zwei Menschen unterschiedlicher Herkunft / Hautfarbe**

victim *n*	**Opfer**
fall victim to sb/sth *v*	**Opfer von jmd./etw. werden**
child abuse [əˈbjuːs] *n*	**Kindesmissbrauch**
go missing *v*	**verschwinden**
= vanish	
slut *n (derog)*	**Schlampe**
▸ slutty	▸ schlampenhaft
Cecil calls her a slut.	Cecil beschimpft sie als Schlampe.

3.3.2 Cecil Walker

stepfather *n*	**Stiefvater**
alcoholic *n*	**Alkoholiker(in)**
molester [məˈlestɚ] *n*	**Peiniger(in)**
child molester	Kinderschänder
molest sb [məˈlest] *v*	**jdn (sexuell) belästigen**
pervert *n*	**Perverse(r)**
abuse sb [əˈbjuːz] *v*	**missbrauchen**
▸ abuse	

3 CHARACTERIZATION

inferiority complex *n*	Minderwertigkeitskomplex
unemployed [ˌʌnɪmˈplɔɪd] *adj*	arbeitslos, ohne Stelle
possessive *adj*	besitzergreifend
be possessive towards / about sb	besitzergreifend gegenüber jdm sein
aggressive *adj*	aggressiv, angriffslustig, streitlustig
violent *adj*	gewalttätig, brutal
ignorant *adj*	unwissend, dumm
remain ignorant of sth	etw nicht kennen
▸ ignorance	▸ Unwissenheit
slimy *adj*	schmierig, widerlich
= repulsive	abstoßend
drunk [drʌŋk] *adj*	betrunken
≠ sober	≠ nüchtern, trocken
get drunk	sich betrinken
be (very) drunk	(stark) betrunken sein

3.3.3 Ina Ott

housewife, -wives [ˈhaʊswaɪf, ˈhaʊswaɪvz] *n*	Hausfrau
volunteer *v*	ehrenamtlich arbeiten, freiwillig melden
charity *n*	Wohltätigkeit
Christian [ˈkrɪstʃən] *n, adj*	Christ(in); christlich
religious *adj*	religiös
prayer *n*	Gebet
▸ pray	▸ beten
Her prayers were answered and Larry finally found a friend.	Ihre Gebete wurden erhört und Larry fand schließlich einen Freund.
stroke *n*	*hier:* Schlaganfall
Alzheimer's (disease) *n*	**Alzheimer**
nursing home *n*	Altersheim, Pflegeheim

CHARACTERIZATION 3

devout [dɪˈvaʊt] *adj*	**fromm, gläubig, devot**
loving *adj*	**liebend, liebevoll**
a loving parent	ein liebevoller Elternteil
affectionate *adj*	**liebevoll, zärtlich**
helpful [ˈhelpfᵊl] *adj*	**hilfreich, hilfsbereit**
independent *adj*	**unabhängig**
strong-willed *adj*	**willensstark**
suffer from sth [ˈsʌfəfrɑːm] *phrasal v*	**an etw leiden, unter etw leiden**
suffer from depression	unter Depressionen leiden
suffer from addiction	süchtig sein
disapprove [ˌdɪsəˈpruːv] *v*	**schlecht finden, missbilligen**
oblivious *adj*	**nichtsahnend**
be oblivious of (to) sth	etw nicht wahrnehmen / nicht bemerken
soothed *adj*	**beruhigt**
▸ soothe	▸ beruhigen
▸ soothing	▸ beruhigend
soothe sb down	jd beruhigen / beschwichtigen

3.3.4 Carl Ott

car-mechanic *n*	**Automechaniker**
racist [ˈreɪsɪst] *adj*	**rassistisch**
manly *adj*	**männlich, wie ein Mann**
strict [strɪkt] *adj*	**streng, konsequent**
= stern	
strict upbringing	strenge Erziehung
aggressive *adj*	**aggressiv**
frigid *adj*	**eisig, kalt, frigide**
malicious [məˈlɪʃəs] *adj*	**boshaft, schadenfroh**
sadistic *adj*	**sadistisch**
menacing *adj*	**bedrohlich**
discourage [dɪˈskɜːrɪdʒ] *v*	**abhalten, entmutigen**
discourage sb from doing sth	jdn davon abbringen, etw zu tun

3 CHARACTERIZATION

affair [əˈfer] *n*	**Affäre, Seitensprung**
be unfaithful to sb *v*	**jdn betrügen**
= cheat on sb	
disappointed [ˌdɪsəˈpɔɪntɪd] *adj*	**enttäuscht**
disappointed in	enttäuscht über, von
laugh [læf] *v*	**lachen**
laugh out loud / aloud	in lautes Gelächter ausbrechen
laugh at sb / sth	über jdn / etw lachen
make sb laugh	jdn zum lachen bringen
burst out laughing	in lautes Lachen ausbrechen, Gelächter anstimmen
beat *v*	**verprügeln**
pass on *phrasal v*	**weitergeben**
tell a story *v*	**eine Geschichte erzählen**
coerce [koʊˈɜːrs] *v*	**zwingen**
coerce sb into doing sth	jdn dazu zwingen, etw zu tun

3.3.5 Alice Jones

beautiful [ˈbjuːt̬ɪfᵊl] *adj*	**schön, sehr gut aussehend** (Anwendung: Frauen und Kinder)
tall [tɔːl] *adj*	**groß (gewachsen)**
black *adj*	**dunkelhäutig**
single parent *n*	**alleinerziehender Elternteil**
single mother	alleinerziehende Mutter
single father	alleinerziehender Vater
independent [ˌɪndɪˈpendənt] *adj*	**unabhängig, selbständig**
≠ dependent *(on)*	≠ abhängig (von)
wary *adj*	**achtsam, wachsam, skeptisch**
protective *adj*	**beschützend**
religious [rɪˈlɪdʒəs] *adj*	**religiös**

CHARACTERIZATION 3

maid *n*	Magd, Hausangestellte
= servant	
send away *v*	wegschicken
struggle *v*	kämpfen, ringen
struggle to make ends meet	Mühe haben, über die Runden zu kommen
▸ struggle for	▸ Kampf um
hard-working *adj*	hart arbeitend
waitress ['weɪtrɪs] *n*	Kellnerin, Serviererin
afford sth *v*	sich etw leisten
scared *adj*	verängstigt
= afraid	= verängstigt
be devoted to one's family *v*	seine Familie sehr lieben, in seiner Familie völlig aufgehen

3.3.6 Angie

pretty ['prɪt̬i] *adj*	hübsch (Anwendung: Frauen und Kinder)
cute [kjuːt] *adj*	süß
light-skinned *adj*	*Afroamerikaner(in) mit heller Hautfarbe*
petite [pəˈtiːt] *adj*	zierlich
pigeon-toed *adj*	sichelfüßig *(Zehenspitzen sind leicht zueinander gedreht)*
natural *adj*	natürlich
pout [paʊt] *v; n*	schmollen, einen Schmollmund machen; Schmollmund
sniffle *v*	schniefen
Emergency Medical Technician (EMT) *n*	Rettungssanitäter
girlfriend ['gɜːrlfrend] *n*	(feste) Freundin
▸ boyfriend	▸ (fester) Freund

caring *adj*	fürsorglich
allegiant *adj*	treu, loyal
lenient *adj*	nachsichtig
investigative *adj*	erforschend, investigativ
likeable *adj*	sympathisch

3 CHARACTERIZATION

3.3.7 Roy French

boss of the local police *n*	**Vorsitzender der örtlichen Polizei**
sheriff *n (higher rank than a constable)*	**Sheriff**
game warden *n*	**Jagdaufseher**
veteran *n (short: vet)*	**Veteran**
A veteran is a former member of the army. French had fought in the Vietnam War.	
smoker [ˈsmoʊkɚ] *n*	**Raucher(in)**
a heavy smoker	starker Raucher, starke Raucherin

---

interview *n*	**Verhör, Befragung**
persuasive *adj*	**überzeugend**
persuasive power	Überzeugungskraft
manipulative *adj*	**manipulativ**
stubborn *adj*	**stur**
determined *adj*	**entschlossen**
callous *adj*	**kaltschnäuzig, abgestumpft**

LITERARY TERMS 4

4.1 Genre

genre [ˈʒɑː(n)rə] n	Gattung
novel n	Roman
family novel n	Familienroman
Southern Gothic novel n	Schauerliteratur, die in den amerikanischen Südstaaten spielt

Crime fiction

Crime fiction is a literary genre that revolves around crimes, criminals and their motives as well as the detection of crime. Much of the genre's fascination is due to the way the narrative unfolds, with the author keeping the reader guessing throughout. Suspense is created by clues that help the reader to find out more and more about the mysteries before the criminal is finally revealed at the end of the story. Crime fiction can be divided in several subgenres, such as **detective fiction** (e.g. **whodunnit**), **legal thrillers** (characters are often lawyers and policemen) or **mystery fiction** (which might even involve the supernatural).

crime fiction n	Krimi(nalliteratur)
detective fiction n = whodunnit	Detektivroman, Krimi
legal thriller n	Justizthriller
mystery novel n	Krimi(nalroman)

Gothic fiction

Gothic fiction (German: *Schauerliteratur*) came into being in the 18th century. Characteristic features of **Gothic novels** are, for example, **mysterious** and **supernatural** elements as well as the themes of horror, terror, death etc. One of the most popular American authors of Gothic fiction was Edgar Allan Poe (1809-1849). Southern Gothic is a subgenre of Gothic literature, but set in the American South. In addition to some of the traditional Gothic elements, such as supernatural or horror elements, these texts often deal with slavery and the repressed history of slavery in the South. Other themes are the grotesque, poverty, violence, or religious issues as well as **eccentric** and morally or physically **deformed** characters.

mysterious adj	geheimnisvoll, mysteriös
supernatural adj	übernatürlich
eccentric [ɪkˈsentrɪk] adj	exzentrisch, ausgefallen
deformed adj	verformt, missgebildet

4 LITERARY TERMS

4.2 Talking about a book

publish sth *v* — etw veröffentlichen
- publication — Veröffentlichung
- publisher — Herausgeber, Verlag

year of publication *n* — Erscheinungsjahr
author *n* — Autor
readership *n* — Leserschaft
recipient *n* — Empfänger (Leser)
review (sth) [rɪˈvjuː] *v* — rezensieren, besprechen
   review books — Bücher rezensieren
   critically review a film — einen Film kritisch rezensieren
- review [ˈrɪvjuː] *n* — Rezension, Besprechung
- write a review — eine Rezension schreiben
- reviewer [rɪˈvjuːɚ] *n* — Rezensent(in), Kritiker(in)

Book report vs. book review

A **book report** is a simple summary of the story's plot with some background information on the author.
A **book review** is a more detailed and critical analysis of the ideas and topics discussed in the text.

criticize [ˈkrɪtɪsaɪz] *v* — kritisieren, rezensieren
- criticism [ˈkrɪtɪsɪzəm] *n* — (Literatur-)Kritik
- critic [ˈkrɪtɪk] *n* — Kritiker(in)

---

narrative *n* — Erzählung, Geschichte, Bericht
epigraph *n* — Epigraph (Inschrift am Anfang eines Buches)
paragraph *n* — Abschnitt, Absatz
line *n* — Zeile
synopsis *n* — Übersicht, Zusammenfassung
   = summary
course of events *n* — Handlungsablauf
   chain of events — Ereigniskette, Handlungskette
clue *n* — Hinweis
plot *n* — Handlung
   plot line — Handlungsverlauf

LITERARY TERMS 4

discourse [ˈdɪskɔːrs] *n, form* — Diskurs; Textabsicht, Textfunktion

  'how' a story is narrated

story *n* — Geschichte, Handlung

  'what' is narrated

Story vs. plot

The term **"story"** refers to the *chronological sequence* of the events and actions in the narrative.
The term **"plot"** refers to the *logical connection between* the events and actions in the narrative.

---

exposition [ˌekspəˈzɪʃᵊn] *n* — Exposition, Erläuterung
turning point *n* — Wende
climax [ˈklaɪmæks] *n* — Höhepunkt
revelation *n* — Aufdeckung, Enthüllung
denouement [dərˈnuːmɑ̃] *n* — Ausgang, Entscheidung, Lösung
  = outcome
setting *n* — Schauplatz, Zeit und Ort der Handlung

---

point of view (p.o.v.) *n* — Perspektive, Sicht
narrative perspective [ˌnerətɪv pəˈspektɪv] *n* — erzählerische Perspektive
  = narrative point of view
  character perspective — Figurenperspektive
  narrator perspective — Erzählerperspektive
limited *adj* — **beschränkt**
  limited perspective — eingeschränkte Perspektive
shift *v* — **verschieben**
  shifting perspectives — wechselnde Perspektiven
narrative technique [tekˈniːk] *n* — **Erzähltechnik**
narrative focus *n* — **Fokus der Erzählung**
parallel narratives *n* — **parallele Erzählstränge**
narrator [ˈnereɪtɚ] *n* — **Erzähler(in)**
  omniscient narrator — allwissender Erzähler
  first-person narrator — Ich-Erzähler
  third-person narrator — auktorialer, personaler Erzähler

4 LITERARY TERMS

omniscient [ɑːmˈnɪʃᵊnt] *adj*	allwissend
reliability *n*	Zuverlässigkeit
▸ reliable	▸ zuverlässig

Narrative situation in *Crooked Letter, Crooked Letter*

The narrative situation in *Crooked Letter, Crooked Letter* could be described as **fractured tandem**. The focus of the chapters alternates between the two main protagonists Larry and Silas (**parallel narratives**) and moves freely in time and space. The reader has to figure out the chronology of events by herself or himself and be alert to any clues and puzzle pieces that later fall into place.

language [ˈlæŋgwɪdʒ] *n*	Sprache
diction [ˈdɪkʃᵊn] *n, uncount*	Wortwahl, Diktion
register [ˈredʒɪstɚ] *n*	sprachliches Register, Sprachebene
formal register	formales Sprachregister
dialect [ˈdaɪəlekt] *n*	Dialekt
drawl *n*	gedehnte Aussprache, breiter Dialekt
Southern drawl	
vernacular [vɚˈnækjələ] *n*	Umgangssprache
dialog (AE) [ˈdaɪəlɑːg] *n* (dialogue (BE))	Dialog

LITERARY TERMS 4

Richness of language: verbs expressing movement	
tumble	purzeln
limp	humpeln
sneak	schleichen
fidget	fummeln, hantieren
fumble	herumfummeln
dodge	ausweichen, sich entziehen,
crouch	hocken, kauern, sich ducken
stumble	stolpern
creep	kriechen
crawl	robben, krabbeln
lurch	torkeln, schwanken

poetic [poʊˈetɪk] *adj* — **poetisch, dichterisch**
  poetic devices — poetische Stilmittel
figurative [ˈfɪɡjəreɪtɪv] *adj* — **figurativ, bildlich**
  figurative language — Bildsprache, Symbolsprache
literal [ˈlɪtərəl] *adj* — **wörtlich**
  take sth literally — etw wörtlich nehmen
vivid *adj* — **lebhaft, anschaulich**
  vivid language — lebendige Sprache
  vivid imagination — lebhafte Fantasie
blunt *adj* — **unverblümt, direkt**
ambiguous [æmˈbɪɡjʊəs] *adj* — **zweideutig, mehrdeutig**
  ≠ unambiguous, clear — ≠ eindeutig
  ambiguous feelings — gemischte Gefühle
  ambiguous wording — missverständlicher Wortlaut
appropriate *adj* — **geeignet, angemessen**
  = suitable
  ≠ inappropriate — ≠ ungeeignet, unangemessen
  appropriate behavior — angemessenes Verhalten
  It's difficult to find the appropriate words in this matter. — Es ist schwierig, die richtigen Worte für diese Angelegenheit zu finden.

4 LITERARY TERMS

Text analysis

Useful phrases:

the reader learns sth about = is given an account of sth = gets to know sth, sb	der Leser erfährt etw über
the reader experiences sth	der Leser erlebt etw
the reader witnesses sth	der Leser wird Zeuge von etw
the narrator takes the reader back in time	der Erzähler führt den Leser in die Vergangenheit
the novel is set in (time, place)	Das Geschehen spielt in (...)
the novel is set against the backdrop of ...	der Roman spielt vor dem Hintergrund ...
the plot gains momentum	die Handlung beschleunigt sich
the plot moves ahead, on	die Handlung läuft weiter
sb, sth gives the reader a sense of impending doom	jmd, etw vermittelt dem Leser den Eindruck, dass ein Unheil naht

....

4.3 Stylistic devices

stylistic [staɪˈlɪstɪk] *adj* — stilistisch
  stylistic devices — Stilmittel
figure of speech *n* — **Redewendung**
foreshadow sth *v* — **etw. vorandeuten**
  = prolepsis
allusion [əˈluːʒ°n] *n* — Anspielung
flashback [ˈflæʃbæk] *n* — Rückblende
  = analepsis
suspense [səˈspens] *n, uncount* — Spannung, Erwartung, Ungewissheit

  = tension
  create suspense — Spannung erzeugen
  moment of suspense — Spannungsmoment
cliffhanger *n* — **offener Ausgang (eines Kapitels)**
intertextuality *n* — **Intertextualität**
  references between texts

LITERARY TERMS 4

telling name *n*	sprechender Name
recur *v*	**wiederholen, wiederkehren**
recurring theme	wiederkehrendes Thema, Leitmotiv

imagery [ˈɪmɪdʒəri] *n*	**Bilder, Bildsprache**
▸ image	
metaphor [ˈmetəfɔːr] *n*	**Metapher, bildlicher Ausdruck**
simile [ˈsɪməli] *n*	**Gleichnis, Vergleich**
alliteration [əˌlɪtəˈreɪʃən] *n*	**Alliteration, Stabreim**
repetition [ˌrepəˈtɪʃən] *n*	**Wiederholung**
euphemism [ˈjuːfəmɪzəm] *n*	**Euphemismus, beschönigender Ausdruck**
exaggeration [ɪɡˌzædʒəˈreɪʃən] *n*	**Übertreibung**
≠ understatement	≠ Untertreibung
▸ exaggerate [ɪɡˈzædʒəreɪt]	▸ übertreiben
irony [ˈaɪrəni] *n, uncount*	**Ironie**
irony of fate	Ironie des Schicksals
▸ ironic*(al)*	▸ ironisch
connotation [ˌkɑːnəˈteɪʃən] *n*	**Nebenbedeutung, Assoziation**
onomatopoeia [ˌɑːnoʊˌmætoʊˈpiːə] *n, no pl*	**Lautmalerei**

NOTES